T0380220

# SOARING
## ON THE
# WINGS
## OF PURPOSE

*Seeds of Wisdom for*
*Purpose Maximization*

DAVID KINGSLEY NIMO

AuthorHouse™
1663 Liberty Drive
Bloomington, IN 47403
www.authorhouse.com
Phone: 833-262-8899

This book is printed on acid-free paper.

ISBN: 978-1-6655-4131-2 (sc)
978-1-6655-4132-9 (e)

Library of Congress Control Number: 2021921370

Print information available on the last page.

Published by AuthorHouse  10/29/2021

authorHOUSE

# CONTENTS

Foreword ............................................................................................................ v

Introduction .................................................................................................. vii

The Purpose ..................................................................................................... 1

The Facilitators of Purpose ...................................................................... 9

About the Author ........................................................................................ 45

# FOREWORD

After reading the Holy Scriptures carefully, we consider that human beings have forgotten their origins and have turned their gaze to the visual, living according to the model and rhythm of their surroundings and imagining that the style and principles of God manifest themselves in what we strive for, feel, see, and experience. In these dark hours of the Last Days, eschatological evidence of this is vividly evident in successful events that rush toward the finish line at unimaginable speed.

The Holy Spirit visited his servant David Kingsley and used him as an instrument to reconcile the divine vision for each of his children. In Psalm 68, it is written, "Your God commands you to be mighty." Commenting on verses 22 to 28 of this text, Matthew Henry says, "The victories with which God blessed David over the enemies of Israel are representations of the victory of Christ, for himself and all believers. Those who make him their own may see him as their God, as their King, for their good, and as a response to their prayers, especially in and through his Word and decrees."

All the rulers and scholars of this world will submit to the kingdom of the Messiah. In verse 28, the people seem to be turning to the king. But the words are for the Savior, his church, and every true believer. We pray that you, O God the Son, will complete your undertaking for us by accomplishing your good work in us.

Surely, we are created in the image and likeness of God and possess unique abilities in our constitution because each of us represents a common but unique species. We have been champions from birth because by His grace and in His foresight, we became winners in a race of 400 million sperm. Therefore, having been selected as champions from the beginning, we must run, walk, act, speak, and live as champions.

God founded us in Christ before we were born (Ephesians 1:4), so in our existence, there is a roadmap for the achievements of each day or the triumph of His goals. "For we are His workmanship, having been created in Jesus Christ for good works, which God has prepared beforehand for us to do" (Ephesians 2:10). As we read these strongly inspired lines, may God help us to bring each one of us back to the purpose for which He created us.


André Choubeu, PhD

# INTRODUCTION

The success of a man is a function of fulfilling his purpose.

A few months ago, on a breezy Saturday evening, David called and told me that he had this heavy assignment ascribed unto him. The Lord had visited him in an encounter after the death of Dr. Myles Munroe and revealed to him that this "great teacher of purpose" had been engaged in writing a series of books that he had never completed. The weight or burden he felt after his encounter with the Lord gave him the conviction that it was a divine task to write this book. When the time was ripe to undertake this divine project, he was immediately led by the Spirit.

Your purpose is to discover what you mean to creation. It keeps you focused by directing your energy and resources to the appropriate quotas where you can make the most of your purpose.

If your purpose is not fulfilled, you will try to gain happiness from other facets of life, such as marriage, family, possessions, or work. But there are some vacuums that only one purpose can fill. Without that purpose, we will try to force other unattained attributes to fill the vacuum—as if trying to put a rectangular pin in a round hole—and we'll ever ponder two questions: What is my exact fit in the world? Why am I here?

Society has grossly misdefined purpose, and many young people are wandering into this misconceived definition, which stems from a combination of inherited values from our upbringing and environmental or social influence. This book will reveal purpose to you as your intended blueprint, by means of which you may understand your unique contribution to the world at large through the lens of the divine will.

Once your purpose is discovered, it should not end there, since a purpose-oriented life creates a generational impact. Dr. Myles Munroe is a perfect example. Although he has translated into Glory, his effect through books still lives on and will last forever. Ultimately, this collection of purpose quotes is for helping us thrive in every facet of life's journey with a sense of assignment, consciousness, purpose, direction, and calling. You need the right words that give you the fullest expressions of the life you are called to live and champion. The quotations provide an overview to convey a comprehensive understanding of what purpose and purposeful commitment are.

Hereby, you are a product of the inventiveness of the Holy Spirit, of insight, brilliance, expressiveness, motivation, originality, and so much more, honed through several hours of refinement and development.

There is certainly no shortage of books to read, but it is worth noting that some books have extraordinarily pertinent knowledge and wisdom that deal with the exact time or epoch at which their relevance can best be expressed. Prophet David Kingsley Nimo believes that this book is a continuation of Dr. Myles Munroe's book *Legacies on Purpose*, which is specifically aimed at the youth of this time.

The originality and authenticity of this book are immaculate. It is a direct product of a place of divine encounter delivered by one of the prophetic leaders of the present generation, instituted by God. Although this book could be read in a few days, I urge you to take the time to reflect on the wisdom of the target quotations and to give it a reason to be a metamorphic reference for life.

With unique content supernaturally downloaded from the sky, *Soaring on the Wings of Purpose* is a signpost for the youth of this generation and the next.


Tebit Makeba Danyella Praise,

PTSMI Nation

# The Purpose

Take advantage of this moment and stretch out in faith, for God has set you apart for an untold success story. In the name of Jesus, you are the next positive surprise in your generation! Yes, you are!

After all, no one is destined by God to fail, but our choices, attitudes, and mindsets are the underlying factors for our outcome in life.

People fail primarily because they want to fail, but you do not have to go down this path. Success is a sum of divine sovereignty and human responsibility. Act now!

There is power in atmosphere. The atmosphere in which we live determines our inspiration, which in turn ignites creativity in us. Creativity is the breeding ground for productivity, and productivity is the wheel of global impact.

Unlock the impulse of your dominant passion. God has wired humanity with an infinite elasticity of potential to actualize and shape the course of the future.

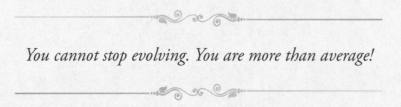

*You cannot stop evolving. You are more than average!*

Your present circumstance could simply be a strategic gift of transformation from God to promote the fulfillment of your purpose and enable you to experience the acts and expressions of divine grace.

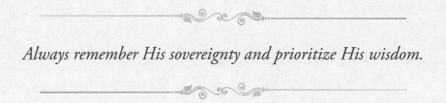

*Always remember His sovereignty and prioritize His wisdom.*

Know the supremacy of divine purpose. Our essential value as human beings reflects our origin and purpose of creation. Therefore, the measure of our full stature and dignity is revealed in the credibility of our Creator's value system, not in the limited understanding of human views.

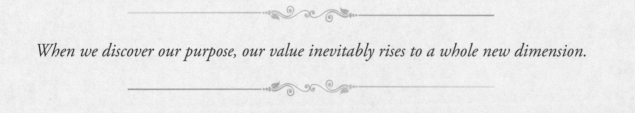

*When we discover our purpose, our value inevitably rises to a whole new dimension.*

Enroll in the school of divine purpose. God's class of purpose is a special, strategic time in our lives in which we are unconsciously led to teachings of maturity by the necessity of the pain that comes from the joy of bad decisions and the deception of ignorance.

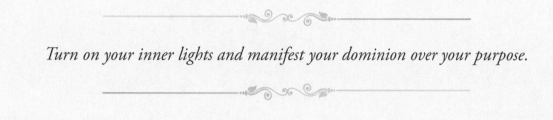

*Turn on your inner lights and manifest your dominion over your purpose.*

Be aware of the hidden wheels of purpose. When divine inspirations collide with human determination on the trajectory of light, acceleration for significance becomes the champion of the day.

*Set your inner wheels of inspiration and determination rolling!*

Your relevance lies in your purpose. Those who are oblivious of their purpose will inevitably live as a shadow of their divine reality.

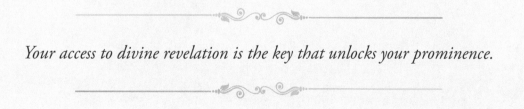

*Your access to divine revelation is the key that unlocks your prominence.*

Beware of the enemies of purpose. The most dangerous neutralizer of a purposeful life is not conspicuous.

—————————————— ⌘ ——————————————

*Pray for grace, discipline, and positive defiance at the altar of prayer.*

—————————————— ⌘ ——————————————

Your purpose will announce you to your generation. Those who live according to their purpose respond positively to the urgency of the present generation and advocate the cause worth dying for as their legacy.

—————————————— ⌘ ——————————————

*The price of a failed purposed life is too high to experience.*

—————————————— ⌘ ——————————————

Improve purpose. Our God-given purpose can be metaphorically equated with a hidden treasure in the dust of oblivion. However, when the light of revelation is kindled, a hero, a pioneer will emerge.

—————————————— ⌘ ——————————————

*Institutionalization is God's transformative philosophy for excellence.*

Knowing your purpose is direction to your progress. True meaning and satisfaction in life can only be achieved on the canvas of a fulfilled purpose, which can also be classified as a life well lived.

*A goal-oriented life is the mother of all achievements.*

Purpose thrives on the wings of gratitude. Every exponential stage of growth on our journey of divine purpose can be traced within the confines of a gratitude mindset.

*A grateful lifestyle will inevitably collide with divine inspiration and revelation.*

Heed the behavior of purpose orientation. The contrast between those who fail miserably and those who leave their mark in the sands of time and eternity revolves around their sense of responsibility, intentionality, and self-discipline.

*Irresponsibility facilitates liability and morbidity.*

God's intentions are intertwined with His purpose. Our divine purpose is the underpinning stream of principles, which guarantees global recognition even in difficult settings.

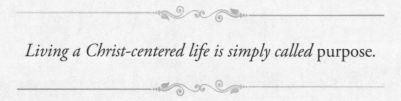

*Living a Christ-centered life is simply called* purpose.

*Purpose and process are inextricably linked. It is our reflection and enlightenment that trigger the idea of relinquishing our willpower completely to be refined by the vicissitudes of life for the goodwill of our purpose.*

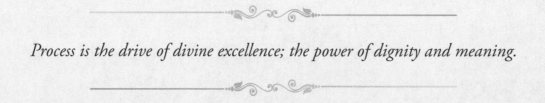

*Process is the drive of divine excellence; the power of dignity and meaning.*

Integrity is the first ally of purpose. The power of integrity is an invisible shield and guardian angel for divine purposes—through its dynamism, our composure and safety become a solid foundation for a swift soaring of our destiny.

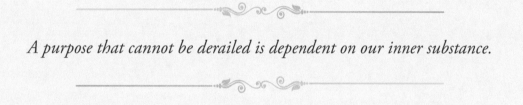

*A purpose that cannot be derailed is dependent on our inner substance.*

Your environment shapes your purpose. The dynamism of an atmosphere of positive influence is the beacon of hope for a purpose caught in an oppressed setting.

*Our imaginative and associative environment contributes significantly to our belief system.*

# THE FACILITATORS OF PURPOSE

Faith is the eye of purpose. An effective purpose is built in the terrain of adversity and trials in life, where absolute trust in God is what instructs our execution of decisions for success and fulfillment.

*Every light encounter triggers result-oriented faith.*

Resilience is a reliable companion of our purpose. It is God's honorable responsibility to guide and keep surveillance over his intentions, interests, and treasures invested in his creation. Ironically, we must proactively cultivate authentic habits that will harness the strength for our inner resistance and against the deceptions of temporal pleasures that derail the focus of our mission and goals.

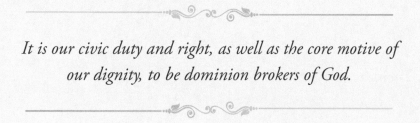

*It is our civic duty and right, as well as the core motive of
our dignity, to be dominion brokers of God.*

Grace divine is our most effective balance in the school of purpose. Why worry when God has planned for and established you from eternity in the parameters of his sovereignty for the fulfilment of your destiny?

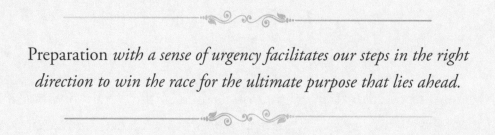

Preparation *with a sense of urgency facilitates our steps in the right direction to win the race for the ultimate purpose that lies ahead.*

You cannot fail when you are on the path of your purpose: If we allow our emotions to drive us, our sensitivity will rob us of lifelong opportunities designed to reward the fruit of our efforts.

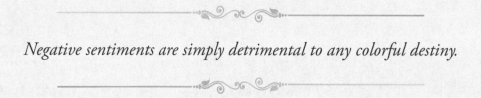

*Negative sentiments are simply detrimental to any colorful destiny.*

Opportunity is time sensitive when it comes to maximizing your purpose to the fullest. Every challenge we encounter in the arena of our quest for excellence brings hidden and endless opportunities.

*It is your exposure that opens your possibilities, and your risk guarantees you an unusual return.*

When purpose collides with affliction, know that the all-wise God, in his omissions, has shaped our lives and greatness to be born within the confinement of painful transitions that conform us to his nature of empathy.

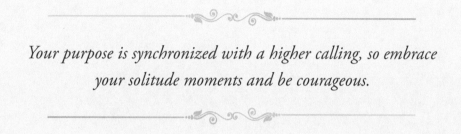

*Your purpose is synchronized with a higher calling, so embrace your solitude moments and be courageous.*

Build your purpose on positive imagination. When we unleash faith and imagine a higher purpose, we unconsciously forge an invisible alliance with the forces of eternity for the next coming attraction of God on earth.

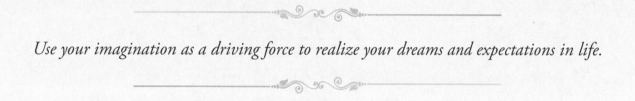

*Use your imagination as a driving force to realize your dreams and expectations in life.*

Faith and fear are the underlying factors of your fulfillment of purpose. Why do you imagine the worst that can manifest when God has divinely wired you to soar like the eagles of your generation? You are more than your best achievement!

*Your next breakthrough will be initiated by God, inspired by the Holy Spirit, and Jesus-centered.*

The superpower of purpose is empathy. A deliberately lived life will inevitably embody an influential legacy for generations that have not yet been born.

---

*When purpose is carefully pursued, it increases the dignity of our personality.*

---

The seed of purpose will break the cycle of generational limitation. It requires personal responsibility with a courageous attitude to reinforce a defiant belief in soaring over the invisible walls of hindrance that surround the realization of one's life purpose.

---

*Dare to kindle your innate urge for change in the right direction.*

---

31. Let your life be driven by a focused purpose. A purpose cultivated in a value-oriented environment is highly formed to attract wealth and honor as a reward of appreciation.

---

*Your inherent gift is merely a tool to accomplish your task;*
*sharpen up by staying on the pulse of time.*

---

My purpose is a timeless treasure. Honesty and nobility certainly reflect those who engage their purpose effectively in the arena of humanity.

*You cannot pay the price of sacrifice and not be hailed as a hero.*

Every purpose must pass the discipline test. The purpose of man can never be derailed if godliness is instilled in his belief system as a central value.

*Your mission is to accomplish God's discharge assignment in the earth realm.*

Emotional stability is the anchor of purpose. Human souls thrive in a realm of absolute serenity and joy, where inspiration lays the groundwork for passion to blossom, enhancing aspirations and visions in all their fullness.

*Create an imaginative concept of endless possibilities and speak those possibilities into motion.*

Pride is a silent destroyer of our purpose. A life founded on the substance of humility and gratitude will exceed expectations of human predictability regardless of the prevailing obstacles.

———————◦❦◦———————

*There is no ascension without submission* (Jesus's encounter with John the Baptist).

———————◦❦◦———————

The pool of knowledge is the gymnasium of purpose. Where wisdom leads or governs our purpose, there are no obstacles or limitations, on our part, to prominence.

———————◦❦◦———————

*The global economy of purpose thrives on the currency of knowledge.*

———————◦❦◦———————

My purpose is a platform of servitude and not a personal privilege. There's no overly high cost to pay when a man falls in love with his purpose.

———————◦❦◦———————

*When a man falls in love with his purpose, there is no excessive price he cannot pay.*

———————◦❦◦———————

A purpose-oriented family is a solid rock of humanity. True love affirms our trust and enriches our sense of intrinsic value, especially when the audacity of our purpose is challenged by self-doubt and rejection.

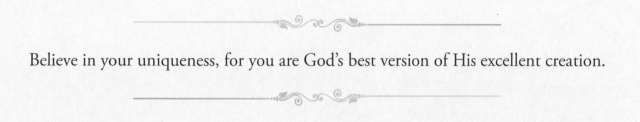

Believe in your uniqueness, for you are God's best version of His excellent creation.

See your purpose through the lens of your creator. Our perceptions in life are extremely vital. They may either be an emancipator and amplifier of our confidence or imprisoner of our dreams.

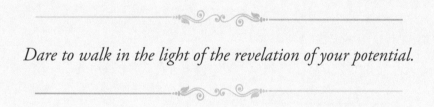

*Dare to walk in the light of the revelation of your potential.*

Systematic discipline is required for the ascendancy of our purpose. Those who dare to align their purpose with the power of integrity will leave an indelible mark in their respective fields of endeavor or assignment.

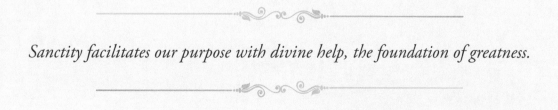

*Sanctity facilitates our purpose with divine help, the foundation of greatness.*

When the voice of purpose echoes through time and eternity, it causes a generational change. The difference between those who leave their mark in the sands of time and those who dwell forever in obscurity is connected to the frequency of their hearing or their intuitive consciousness.

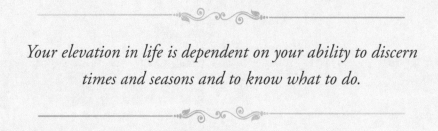

*Your elevation in life is dependent on your ability to discern times and seasons and to know what to do.*

Your purpose and your responsibility coherently head in the same direction. If we cultivate self-discipline by saying yes to delay satisfaction on the path of purpose, then our willpower will be dictated by the choices of our destiny rather than the desires of temporal pleasures.

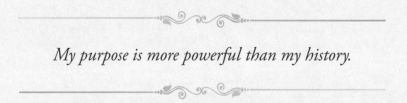

*My purpose is more powerful than my history.*

Your purpose is designed and wired to pave the way. Those who dare to think that their life's mission is much higher than their current circumstances test their potential by going from the valleys to the summit of the mountain and becoming the best version of themselves.

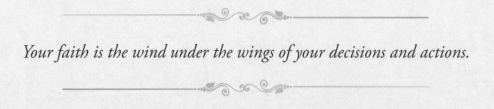

*Your faith is the wind under the wings of your decisions and actions.*

Obscurity is God's birthing place of great purposes. The significance of divine providence over our purpose is to arrange the sovereign times and seasons of life's opportunities and to promote the accomplishment of our predestination in life.

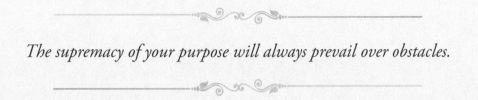

*The supremacy of your purpose will always prevail over obstacles.*

Regardless of the uncertainties of times, your purpose will thrive. If we are to rely on the generosity and thoughtfulness of the all-wise and all-knowing God, then no amount of self-doubt or horrible experience in the past should be able to derail our purpose.

*Your purpose is a divine project with an unspeakable success story.*

Investing quality time in our purpose is not a pointless exercise but, rather, a generational dividend. Our physical, mental, and emotional strength is an invaluable fuel for life. Consequently, we often lack awareness and intentionality. However, investing in our purpose daily maximizes it to the fullest.

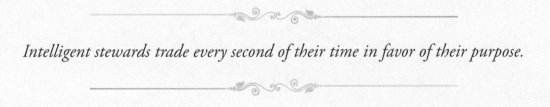

*Intelligent stewards trade every second of their time in favor of their purpose.*

An authentic purpose cannot wear a symbiotic lens (narrow-mindedness). It is an undeniable fact that being diligent in fulfilling our obligations in life in the global space will inevitably bring us great honor. Nonetheless, selflessness must be the motivation for our pursuit of goals.

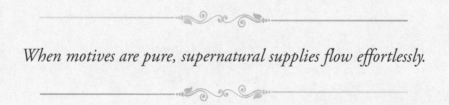

*When motives are pure, supernatural supplies flow effortlessly.*

High value draws the best out of our purpose and stabilizes it. When a leader compromises his conscience due to a lack of focus amid positive influences in the right direction, a generational moment is lost forever.

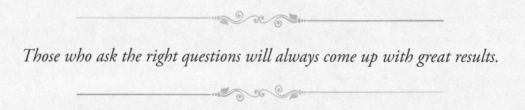

*Those who ask the right questions will always come up with great results.*

Compatibility is reflective in purposeful alliance. Those who make their life choices from the perspective of the higher light for a deeper consciousness are, ironically, aligning themselves for a successful journey into the future.

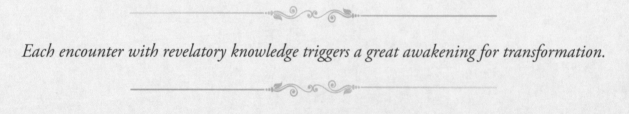

*Each encounter with revelatory knowledge triggers a great awakening for transformation.*

Fulfilling our purpose transforms us into an entity of liberty and a force of change for our generation. The ability to coordinate the awareness of a mission beyond ourselves with a sense of personal responsibility is what propels the actualization of our purpose in motion.

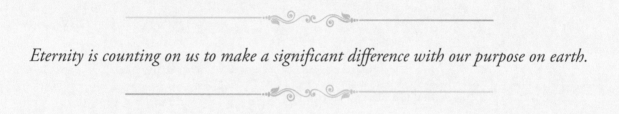

*Eternity is counting on us to make a significant difference with our purpose on earth.*

Until you discover purpose, the driving force of your destiny will be dysfunctional or powerless. If and only if humankind dares to believe that the success of its mission in its global outer space is one of the endless expectations of eternity, our daily decisions will certainly be considered with great care.

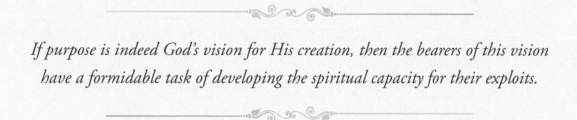

*If purpose is indeed God's vision for His creation, then the bearers of this vision have a formidable task of developing the spiritual capacity for their exploits.*

Each divine purpose is designed to accomplish a multi-generational task. The magnitude of humanity's purpose is a striking reflection of the mystery of its God-innate nature. It is, therefore, irrational for any of us to measure ourselves by social status.

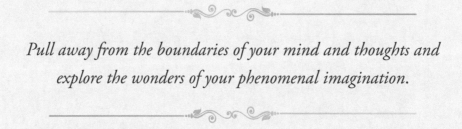

*Pull away from the boundaries of your mind and thoughts and explore the wonders of your phenomenal imagination.*

The realm of positive imagination is a natural habitat for a flourishing purpose. A healthy mindset enhances the realization of a holistic soul and mind, both of which promote an effective purpose.

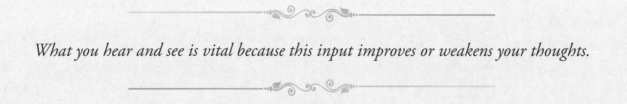

*What you hear and see is vital because this input improves or weakens your thoughts.*

Do not wait for a disobedient or undisciplined person to waste your purpose in life. If you follow your purpose with zeal, you will inevitably outperform your wildest expectations, leaving a generational legacy that will be impossible to erase.

*Why keep waiting when you can determine your destiny with personal commitment and determination?*

Every purposeful woman rejuvenates their beauty in the fountains 🏺 of gratitude and happiness

*Your inner beauty is a priceless treasure never trade it for silver or gold.*

Guard your purpose with all diligence, for it is your only reason for living. Our faith and patience are the essential triggers that inspire our willpower when we dare to climb the ladder of higher devotion and deeper commitment.

*The path of pacesetters is tough but not impossible.*

When our purpose is confronted by the changes of life, faith and the perseverance of hope are needed to maintain confidence in a better tomorrow. Those who heed the call of their purpose have an unimaginable wealth of transformative resources for generations yet to emerge for greater exploits.

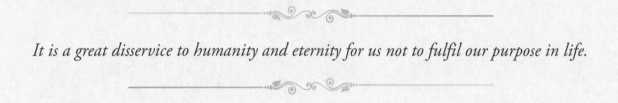

*It is a great disservice to humanity and eternity for us not to fulfil our purpose in life.*

Your purpose is the current that supplies the light of hope and inspiration to your contemporaries, to the voiceless, and to the oppressed. The reason for our existence is often embedded in our transitioning from time to eternity, simply because we are all called for a purpose.

*Dare to believe that you are here for a reason, a season, and a generation.*

59. Your personality is embedded in your purpose, so polish it with an attitude of sincerity and integrity. Just as the human brain and mind are inseparably linked by their coexistence, our decisions and willpower are synonymous with each other—these are the determining factors that facilitate the discovery of our purpose.

*The synergy between a dreaming mind and a willing heart is the secret of great inventors.*

The two most harmful forces that Satan has ever used against the purpose of humankind are laziness and pride. A generation with a narcissistic mindset will eventually belittle the essence of its purpose or trade it for instant gratification.

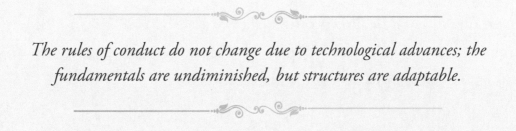

*The rules of conduct do not change due to technological advances; the fundamentals are undiminished, but structures are adaptable.*

Every God-centered purpose will inevitably undergo a journey of purification through the process of fiery trials for character reconstruction and upgrading to standard excellence. A healthy purpose can only be nurtured on the platform of humility, where holiness is highly esteemed as a precursor of achievements.

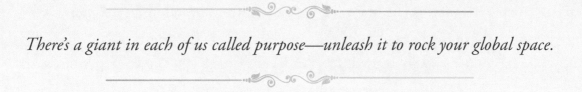

*There's a giant in each of us called purpose—unleash it to rock your global space.*

It's impossible to overestimate the significance of divine purpose. Every divine purpose is associated with the grace to leave an indelible impression on humanity. However, the underlying predictor of its successful execution is practical wisdom.

*If life is a battle, then our purpose is destined to be the target.*

Your purpose should never be drowned by shallow waters because it is founded on the solid rock of God. Shame and failure are not part of purpose. Nevertheless, those who lose their guide of discipline end up in a deplorable manner.

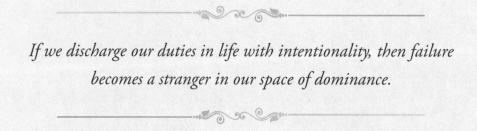

*If we discharge our duties in life with intentionality, then failure becomes a stranger in our space of dominance.*

When our purpose is discovered, the discovery ignites a compelling drive, along with a sense of clarity and the certainty of execution. The inner strength of our purpose is our faith in God, but the muscle of faith must be developed in the gymnasium of our life's struggles.

*The clarity of your purpose is based on the awareness of your purpose.*

The affirmation of your purpose projects confidence and high self-esteem, which enables you to break boundaries and set new standards of excellence. A dream of purpose must be nurtured near the confines of inspiration in order to survive and thrive in seasons of discouragement.

*Intellectual prowess and experiential competence are mandatory for a purpose of higher callings.*

Understanding the grace factor of purpose fuels our belief system with a winning mentality. Ultimately, God's essential aim for humanity is to serve His purposes in the earthly kingdom. In other words, He is ready to invest His divine resources to facilitate the fulfillment of His purposes concerning His creation.

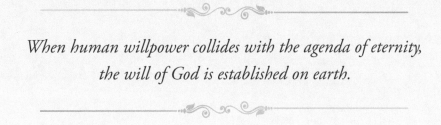

*When human willpower collides with the agenda of eternity,*
*the will of God is established on earth.*

It's the uniqueness of one's purpose that determines the course of his or her preparation. Every fulfilled purpose is an expression of God's joy and a beacon of hope for the hopeless.

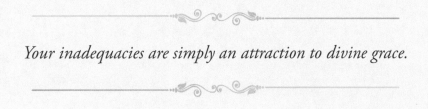

*Your inadequacies are simply an attraction to divine grace.*

25

The longevity of a man's purpose can easily be measured by the strength of his character, understanding, and compassion and, lastly, of his ability to heed wise counsel. Any decision made based on compromise or ignorance is a construction of failure and a self-imposed limitation of the potentials of our God-given purposes.

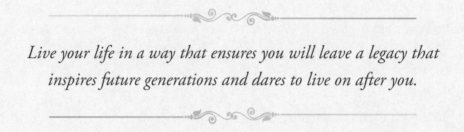

*Live your life in a way that ensures you will leave a legacy that inspires future generations and dares to live on after you.*

The power of positive utterance is a great stabilizer of purpose. Those who discern when to remain silent 🔔 will erect an invisible wall of defense around their purpose against hostilities and disputes.

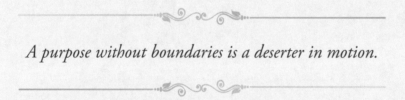

*A purpose without boundaries is a deserter in motion.*

Every purposeful learning has its price and a process of painful losses. Every purposeful global leadership reflects such prerequisites of strategic positioning, systematic structure, and emotional staying power for consistent delivery of authentic results.

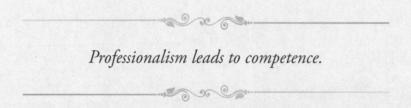

*Professionalism leads to competence.*

The only reason for certainty and security amid uncertainty is your purpose. Our ability to consolidate self-discipline and strong will creates a defense mechanism that enables you to live a purposeful life.

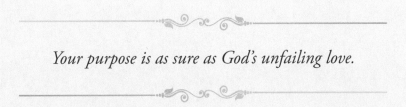

*Your purpose is as sure as God's unfailing love.*

Understanding the realm and the fictionality of your purpose is a leverage for exploits. The parallel truth of the capacities and functions between moonlight and sunlight is synonymous with our goals and their responsibilities, activities, and seasons of execution or performance.

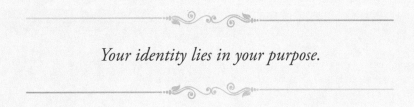

*Your identity lies in your purpose.*

The discovery of our purpose leads to strategic positioning and distinctive roles. Purposeful men and women live their lives in the realm of positive expectation, despite the obvious challenges surrounding their environments.

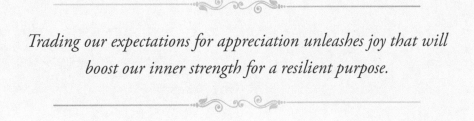

*Trading our expectations for appreciation unleashes joy that will*
*boost our inner strength for a resilient purpose.*

Personal dignity and spiritual immunity are byproducts of executing purpose. When we pursue our life goals with due care and intelligence, our inherent nature of domination inevitably becomes a force of courage to do the impossible.

*Philosophical transition is a necessity of purpose.*

You cannot build a life based on a culture of purpose without flexibility. God in His omissions intentionally uses His miraculous deeds and His tried and tested methodology to equip our purposes for extraordinary accomplishments to His glory.

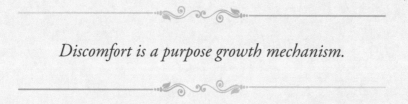

*Discomfort is a purpose growth mechanism.*

The audacity of hope is a divine life force of purpose. The unadulterated integrity of God's faithfulness should be our assurance of our faith in His endless possibilities.

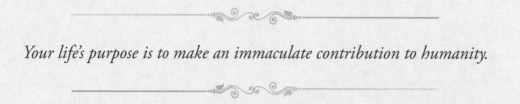

*Your life's purpose is to make an immaculate contribution to humanity.*

The capacity of your purpose is based on the weight of responsibility eternity places on your potential. It is the inadequacies of our lives that illuminate the elegance in the beauty of the uniqueness of our personal untold purpose stories.

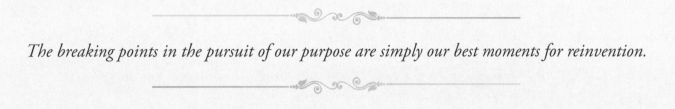

*The breaking points in the pursuit of our purpose are simply our best moments for reinvention.*

Anchor your purpose with internal evidence in the endless hope of God's grace. If you fail to consolidate the ancient wisdom of godliness and transformative knowledge of civic education as a fundamental skill, then the ultimate potential of your purpose will be trapped in the state of perpetual mediocrity.

*Your purpose is God's project in progress.*

Understanding the cyclical factors of divine purpose improves its reinvention, if necessary. It takes a bold and courageous heart, along with an unusual resilience, to weather the sudden storms of adversity that arise on our journey of a purposeful mission. So ignore distractions and manage your emotions because you are almost there.

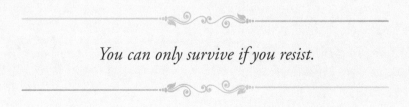

*You can only survive if you resist.*

What do you do when your purpose is stagnant? Those who follow the eagles' 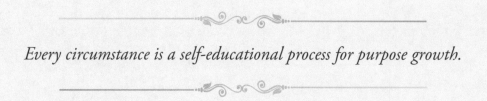 strategy of systemic refreshment by filling up the tank of their mind, soul, and body will certainly rejuvenate their emotional well-being, guaranteeing a cutting-edge purpose, along with high-level performance.

*Every circumstance is a self-educational process for purpose growth.*

A calm soul is a firm foundation for a shining purpose. The battle of the soul is the tipping point of satanic wars against the bearers of great goals. Those who have founded their spirituality on an intimate relationship with the Almighty God are shielded with the wings of His angelic powers.

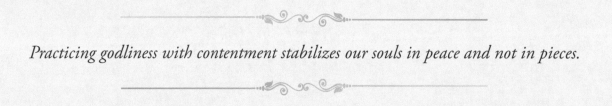

*Practicing godliness with contentment stabilizes our souls in peace and not in pieces.*

Your purpose could be extremely challenging, but it cannot be defeated under any circumstances. Always remember, the giants along the way of your destiny have been predestined to reveal the power of your divine ability and to proclaim you to your generation.

*It is impossible to distinguish challenges from championing your purpose.*

Growing into the highest version of your purpose can be a daunting task, but it won't be impossible if determination is your companion. When God's purpose for our lives becomes our delightsome duty, then He is obligated to endorse us as global icons in His kingdom.

*You cannot be disappointed if you dream of purpose, think of purpose, and live by purpose.*

The power of perseverance is the wind under the wings of those who are designed according to His purpose: You're on a flight of divine purpose with a divine intention, and the Lord of the universe is the captain on board. So relax and enjoy the journey of your destiny.

*Your safe arrival is guaranteed by the supremacy of God.*

The lifeline of our purpose is our spirituality in motion. People's inner strength is their stronghold of trust. It also inspires their dominant passion for the hidden wheels of their destiny.

*Our purpose's mission statement is predicated on the design of our destinies.*

The signs and testimonies that confirm every divine purpose are simply inexplicable but also indisputable. On our journey of greatness, faith and patience become the compass of the ship 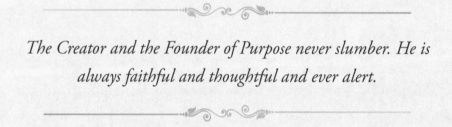 of destiny as we navigate difficult waters and turbulent times.

*The Creator and the Founder of Purpose never slumber. He is always faithful and thoughtful and ever alert.*

The invisible anchors of purpose are simply core values oriented toward godliness. Visionary leaders who set out in their respective fields of activity reflect the characteristics of ironed will and dogged focus. Because of these high virtues, there is no option or thought worth circumventing the blending and polishing processes of their divinely ordained purposes as they head toward their shining moments of destiny.

*There're no shortcuts to a mountaintop 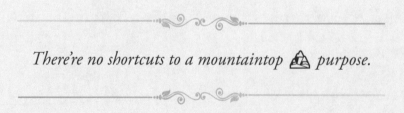 purpose.*

Living a life of orderliness is the corner stone or the bedrock of purpose. Those who allow the seasons of delay and despair to influence decisions in their pursuit of goals will no doubt find themselves in the valley of regret, due to missed opportunities and missed moments of great significance.

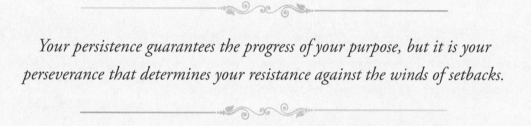

*Your persistence guarantees the progress of your purpose, but it is your perseverance that determines your resistance against the winds of setbacks.*

Joyfulness enriches and immunizes purpose from discouragement, whilst disappointments breed despondency in the face of its progress. The predisposition to optimism is a nonnegotiable objective for two main reasons—firstly, to defy negativism and, secondly, to improve our confidence by imagining opportunities in the face of inequality and gloominess.

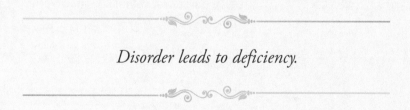

*Disorder leads to deficiency.*

The sovereignty of God is the sponsor of purpose-personified leaders. Looking at the historicity of men and women with remarkable determination, those who have positively shaped their generations in a transformative way, one can, therefore, conclude that the grace of the invisible hand of God is their shield of preservation and their inner strength.

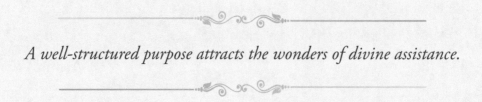

*A well-structured purpose attracts the wonders of divine assistance.*

Your purpose is important because you are indispensable when it comes to its execution. Recognizing and celebrating our uniqueness in life is simply not enough. It is a periphery of an exciting adventure of positive surprises with timeless treasures.

*Unleash your imagination and engage your curiosity for an*
*amazing revelation of your glorious purpose.*

Your purpose is the ☆ star of your family success story. Those who approach life with perception and insight simply say, "Your prophecy in life is the script of your purpose, and your daily experiences develop like the story of a divine film called *Destiny*."

*You're God's instrument ℘ of purpose. Believe it and do it.*

Love is the universal characteristic language of divine purpose. It is of the utmost importance that every successful purpose cultivates a healthy philosophy and a holistic belief system as a formidable foundation to withstand the adversities and insecurities of life.

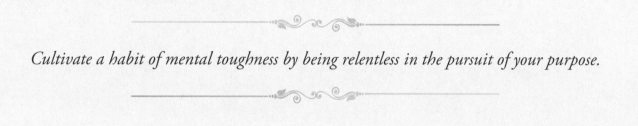

*Cultivate a habit of mental toughness by being relentless in the pursuit of your purpose.*

Every effective purpose is an offensive weapon of God against the works of Satan. Nothing neutralizes or undermines the audacity of purpose like self-aggrandizement and the love of money.

*The sharpening of discernment activates immunity against susceptibility and deception.*

All experiential knowledge authentically preserves purpose. Whoever wants to swing on the wings of his or her God-given purpose in life must first create a conscious and systematic order that works coherently with a holistic structure to increase efficiency in his or her respective career.

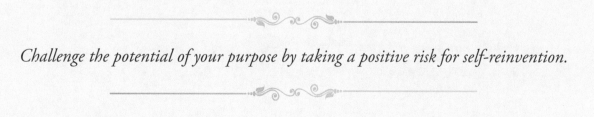

*Challenge the potential of your purpose by taking a positive risk for self-reinvention.*

The factors of a successful purpose can be discovered only in our quest for godliness. Divine grace and mercy will always compensate for the fiscal disadvantages that affect the purpose of humanity, regardless of race or gender.

*A purposeful prayer is already an answered petition and a resounding testimony.*

The emergence of transitioning of purpose is inevitable, irrespective of our state of readiness. Every successful purpose has two major footprints, in a form that evolves from personal growth to the position of being recognized as the embodiment of institution in the global space.

*Evolution from the seed stage to a forest* 🌳 *is God's anticipation for all lives.*

The sanctity of freedom is the hallmark of purpose. Every character flaw facilitates a self-imposed limitation against the driving force of our purpose in all ramifications of life in general.

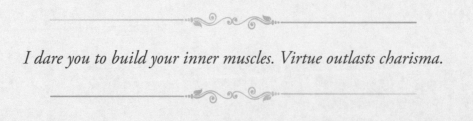

*I dare you to build your inner muscles. Virtue outlasts charisma.*

Your personality is deeply wired as a single-minded being on a mission of influence. Regardless of our family's pedigrees, divine providence determines the fulfilment our destinies.

*When our purpose is recognized, purity, wealth, and prominence become our rewards.*

A purpose of resilience is based on true love and great faith in the endless hope of God's sovereignty: It's absolutely a fair for every carrier of great purpose to be tested with stressful situations in the parameters of extreme pressure under the law's nature.

*Pain generates power and passion for purpose development.*

Your rewards and recognition in life are synchronized with your purpose. If there is a struggle worth fighting and dying for, it is for an undeniable reason—humans were designed for dominance.

*The sacrifice of the cross* † *is the full measure of the value of your purpose.*

Pain and purpose are inextricably linked. Every painful lesson learned on the path of self-discovery is a positive instigator of change, but targeted action is needed to turn it into a generational movement.

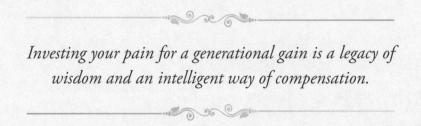

*Investing your pain for a generational gain is a legacy of wisdom and an intelligent way of compensation.*

Passion always points to purpose. The discovery of the pathways to maximizing our purpose is primarily an intrinsic journey of curiosity in our self-analysis.

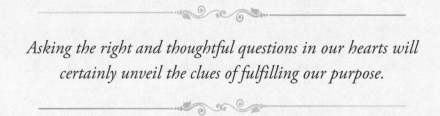

*Asking the right and thoughtful questions in our hearts will certainly unveil the clues of fulfilling our purpose.*

Conflicts and triumphs are refinements of purpose. The resilience of a blooming soul reflects single-mindedness and willpower that has ultimately undergone a disciplinary transformation process.

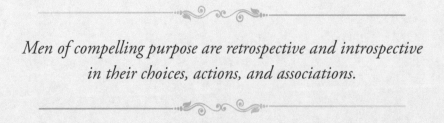

*Men of compelling purpose are retrospective and introspective in their choices, actions, and associations.*

Our purpose is God's economic wheels. If generosity and empathy are forged as a sacred alliance with purpose, it will inevitably create unlimited resources for the good of humanity.

*Sacrifice is always a game changer.*

Servitude and selflessness are the two indelible marks of a purposeful life. The essential value of a person's existence can easily be quantified by the significant contributions he or she has made to societies and individuals through the platforms of his or her abilities, talents, and inherent treasures placed at his or her disposal by his or her creator.

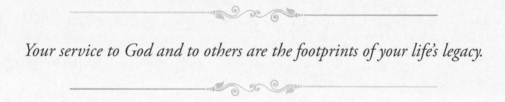

*Your service to God and to others are the footprints of your life's legacy.*

You are embedded with a purposeful seed for the fruitfulness of your unique assignment. The purpose of civic education is to polish destinies and shine the light on the treasure of eternity in each one of us.

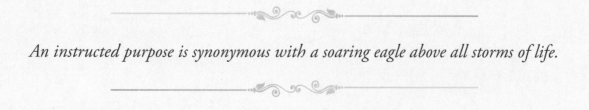

*An instructed purpose is synonymous with a soaring eagle above all storms of life.*

The human brain is full of infinite treasures for creative purposes. Without an illumination of the light of divine knowledge, the phenomenal faculties and functions of the human spirit will slumber in its purposeful use of creation.

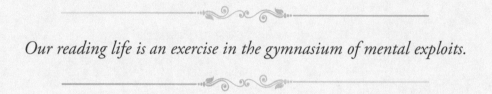

*Our reading life is an exercise in the gymnasium of mental exploits.*

Its easier to be popular than to be purposeful. The influence of purposeful living sets a standard of meaning that generations can emulate, while a pleasure-oriented lifestyle creates shadows of nobility and authenticity.

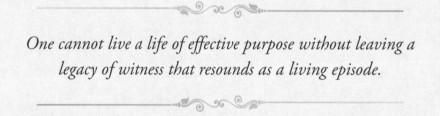

*One cannot live a life of effective purpose without leaving a legacy of witness that resounds as a living episode.*

The season of purpose is decisive for its execution and influence. Looking at a purpose through the lens of sacrifice creates awareness of strategic discipline that strengthens our focus, especially in moments of discouragement and distractions.

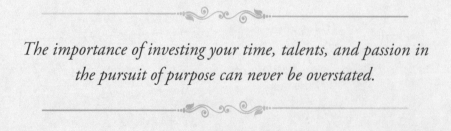

*The importance of investing your time, talents, and passion in the pursuit of purpose can never be overstated.*

Those who have marginalized the value of purpose never advance beyond the cage of comfort. Believing that your life is an essential value and that it is purposely designed to accomplish a unique mission beyond human understanding is a philosophy of heroism and the mentality of champions.

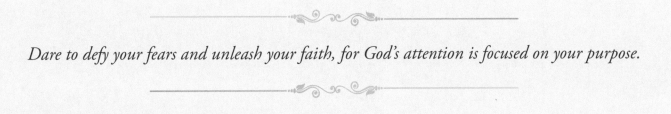

*Dare to defy your fears and unleash your faith, for God's attention is focused on your purpose.*

Nothing else matters to eternity than your purpose. The idea of the purpose of life was conceived in the grand thought of God, with the motive of pure love for greatness and serving humanity with an excellent spirit.

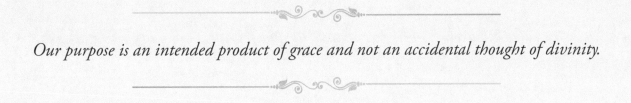

*Our purpose is an intended product of grace and not an accidental thought of divinity.*

Guard your purpose with due diligence, for it is the only reason and essence of life. A diligent spirit sets up a platform of impact for those whose lives are tuned to the frequency of purpose pursuits.

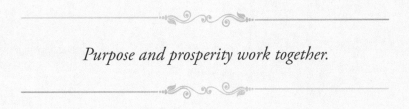

*Purpose and prosperity work together.*

Men with a strong sense of purpose excel at the smallest of tasks. Many people fail to believe in and work with life's developing processes because they expect to have a glimmer of achievement tied to their great callings..

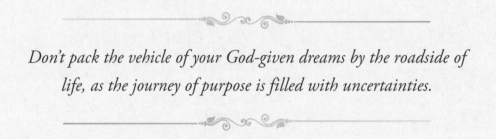

*Don't pack the vehicle of your God-given dreams by the roadside of life, as the journey of purpose is filled with uncertainties.*

Character equity is central to divine purpose. For purpose to be attained in the pedestal realm of significance and longevity, it must be sustained by the currency of faith and charity.

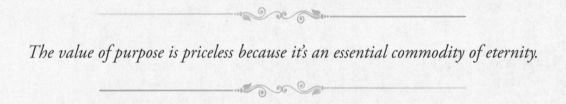

*The value of purpose is priceless because it's an essential commodity of eternity.*

The mountain 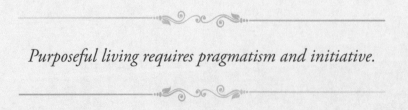 of ignorance is an invisible barrier to the fruition of purpose. A well-blended purpose is an amalgamation of intellectual efficiency and a light of experiential knowledge.

*Purposeful living requires pragmatism and initiative.*

Your purpose was designed and founded on the canvass of love. The results of our efforts towards the actualization of our divine purpose are absolutely guaranteed on god's integrity

*A principled oriented life flocks together with purpose mindedness.*

Giving your purpose undivided attention is a worthwhile investment for a lifetime breakthrough. Before we were formed in the thoughts  of our creator, he embedded the dream seed of purpose into the core of beings, to express the magnificence of his abilities in our humanity

*The dignity of labor inflates the value of purpose in all ramifications of life.*

*The gravity of purpose draws us towards the center of all things, with a seldom certainty and peace unspeakable. Every divine call to purpose is certainly beyond ourselves, our society, and beyond the climate of human opinion or the prejudice and the skepticism in which we live*

*Soaring on the wings of purpose simply means breaking the limits and living life to the fullest.*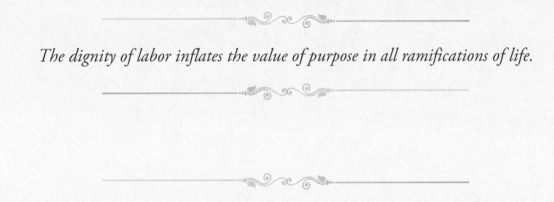

Neglecting your seed of purpose is simply denying your generation a tool or a transformation solution. The endless rewards of great stewardship of purpose include an alliance of consistent diligence and an initiative-oriented mentality or mindset.

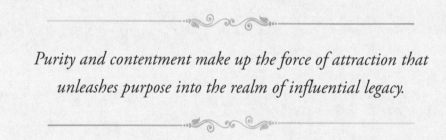

*Purity and contentment make up the force of attraction that unleashes purpose into the realm of influential legacy.*

# About the Author

**DAVID KINGSLEY NIMO** is a Ghanaian-born missionary, preacher, author, orator, and businessman based in Belgium. He followed both the formal path of formation and that of divine care, and his deep commitment to the Lord began as an intercessor at the International Central Gospel Church. From there, he gained worldwide influence, and his passionate heart and zeal for missionary work is reflected in his journey to several countries in Africa, Europe, and the United States of America, where his influence was felt. He is a sought-after speaker with a unique message that focuses on purity, godliness, and expediency and aims to give birth to visionaries of the generation. He works with various Christian leaders, clergy, and envoys, transcending denominational and cultural barriers.

Currently, David is the founder of David Nimo Ministries. He loves to write phenomenal, thought-provoking, and inspiring quotations on various keynotes. He is also the visionary of The Prayer Alarm Devotional, and he aspires to write more articles and books documenting the lives of young people who have lost track of themselves and are living by God's will in order to become aligned with His will and manifest their purpose.

Printed in the United States
by Baker & Taylor Publisher Services